THE PROMISE

By Chavi Diamond

Illustrations by Luda Stekol

Dedicated to my parents, Chaim & Frida Lieberman A"H, true heroes of their time.
I was lucky enough to personally hear from them the real TRUTH.

A gift to my grandchildren & generations to come.
Because we have to care.

A long, long time ago, in a big, beautiful house in Hungary...

There lived three little Jewish princesses:
Vera, Suzy, and me, Eva.

I was the oldest, and I loved looking after my sisters.
My mother always said I was her best little helper!

We had a wonderful life in our big, beautiful house
near our family and friends.

But one day in 1944,
strange and frightening things began to happen.

A huge army came marching into our town from Germany.

Its leader was a very bad man named Hitler.

I thought Hitler was a lot like Pharaoh in Egypt.

He hated every Jewish person in the whole world.

He made us sew yellow stars on our beautiful, warm, princess coats.

We and our friends weren't allowed to go out and play
like the non-Jewish children.

One day Hitler made us leave our big, beautiful house.

His terrible soldiers, the Nazis, only let us take one suitcase each,
for everything we wanted to keep!

We each carried our one bag into
a huge, dirty building.

It used to be a factory, but now the one
room was meant to be a home for us and
all of our Jewish friends and relatives.

All we could see were mattresses.

It was hard to live in an empty factory!

It was always crowded, and there was never quite enough food.

Still, we were all Jewish and we all worked together
to keep the *mitzvos** as well as we could.

We lived there together with our mommy and daddy for weeks,
but then things got even worse.

One day, those horrible soldiers came back,
and made us all get into one very crowded train!

The train brought us all to a frightening place called
a Concentration Camp.

At the concentration camp,
people were sent to different places.

My sister Vera and I were separated
from the rest of our family.

As my mother and Suzy were taken away from us,
I heard her say, "Watch over your sister!
Promise you'll bring her home safe!"

Vera and I stayed together.

We stayed together when they cut off all our hair.

14

We stayed together when
the Nazi took away what
remained of our beautiful clothing
and gave us rags instead.

We stayed together when
they took away our *siddur**
and we could only pray
what we knew by heart.

*prayer book   15

We stayed together on *Tisha B'Av**,
when it was very easy to be sad.

Naturally, we were sad.

**The day we mourn the destruction
of the temple in Jerusalem*

16

And we stayed together when we lost track of the holidays we loved, which was even more sad. But at least we were sad together.

One day the Nazis came in.

They told us that some of us would be chosen
to work in a factory in Germany.
They chose me.

They did not choose Vera.

I didn't know what to do.

I had promised my mother to stay with Vera,
but the Nazis never let anyone argue with them.

We had been separated from our mother,
our father, and our dear little sister.

How could we be separated from each other, too?

The Nazis made us go into the showers and wash ourselves with hoses.

We came out dripping wet, and I was still trying to think.

How could I get Vera to leave this place with me?

She was standing there dry and frightened,
with all of the other dry, frightened girls.

I needed to help her somehow!

Then the soldier watching us left the room for a moment.

My eyes saw a beautiful sight:
the hose we had washed with was still on a bench nearby.

Oh, I was scared, but I knew now what my plan was!

It was now or never.

I snatched up that hose and sprayed water all over every single girl in that room!

Some of them screamed in surprise. Some of them laughed.

And some of them just looked thoughtful.

The soldier heard all the noise and came running back in.

We were all dripping wet and the two groups were mixed together.

"Who did this?!" the soldier shouted.

I closed my mouth and looked down.

No one answered.

There was no time for the Nazis to choose again.

They looked at us carefully, but now that we were all wet, we looked just the same as each other.

"Then they'll all have to go," the soldier said angrily.

And we all did.

Vera and I stayed together.

I had kept my promise.

Our lives in the factory were very difficult.

The work was hard,
we were hungry,
and we missed our family.

At least we were together.

Finally, after many long
and difficult months,
the American soldiers arrived.

They saved us from the factory
and told us we were free.

The Nazis were gone forever.

Some kind people helped us look for our family,
and we did find some relatives.

Our mother, father, along with our dear little Suzy,
were killed.

The years passed.

Vera and I both got married, and moved to America
where we live today.

With G-d's help we raised a new generation of
beautiful Jewish children.

Eva (Lux) Braun

with author Chavi Diamond

Eva (Lux) Braun was born in 1927 to Isaac and Devora Lux in Kosice, Czechoslovakia. She was the first of three daughters. When she was a teenager, her peaceful existence came to an abrupt end.

Eva survived the concentration camps and Nazi brutality with G-d's help, and learned to overcome life's adversities through faith and perseverance. She credits her parents for teaching her how to be a good person, and she rejoices in the beautiful family that she was blessed with.

Eva has shared her story with thousands; speaking candidly of numerous Kristallnacht remembrances to audiences of high school students, volunteering for 15 years as a guide at Yad Vashem, appearing in Oprah's Magazine and in an interview on NBC.

Her memoirs appear in a German chronicle/biography *"Ich War Und Ich Bin Eine Stolze Judin"* (I was and still am a proud Jew), by Anning Lehmensiek. Eva's story has been published in Oprah's anthology of the best 100 stories.

"I am pleased that this book based on my family's life will further promote awareness of the Holocaust. When my grandson was 3 years old, he asked about the numbers on my arm. When I told him that I would explain it to him when he was a little older, he innocently responded, "Oh I know, when you go to a pool or amusement park they stamp your arm so that you can come and go as you please".

Yes...I nodded, this certainly was an exclusive "club" that we belonged to.

Excerpted from

Chaim the Hero

For many months I (Chaim) worked with fellow Jewish Partisans* as we smuggled children out of Camps and into the woods.

We sent many to safety on children transports to Israel…

*A group of brave individuals who banded together to fight against the Nazis

Excerpted from

Escape to Shanghai

After the Yeshiva escaped to China, the Japanese officials in charge were ordered to send them back to Europe.

Upon hearing this terrible news, the Rosh Yeshiva approached the Japanese head officer and said, "Don't think Hitler is going to stop with the Jews. When he's done killing Jews, you're next!"

Upon hearing those words, he let them stay . . .

Note to Parents and Educators:

This book is intended for children of all ages. Whether it is read to them or they read it on their own, children will gain knowledge about the Holocaust and, in some cases, more about their own families' recent history.

While the details of the Holocaust are vitally important to pass down to future generations, it is imperative that you remain sensitive to your child's age and emotional maturity. Some information in this book may be vague in nature in order to avoid exposure to some of the more frightening aspects of our ancestors' history.

Children should be encouraged to ask questions and adults are encouraged to answer with honest, simple responses. Some details in the story may be beyond your child's understanding and may not have to be addressed or embellished upon. However, a more mature or inquisitive child may focus on details in the story or picture. For example: There is a picture of barbed wire, but no mention of it in the story. The number tattooed on Eva's arm might be questioned. You might want to prepare your answers in advance.

In most cases, this story will hit close to home. Parents and educators are encouraged to bring their emotional attachment to the reading in order to fully pass along its message.

Cheryl (Diamond) Weinberger, M.S.Ed.
School Psychologist
Administrative Director of an Early Childhood Program

Granddaughter of a Holocaust Survivor